Occupational Safety and Health Administration

U.S. Department of Labor

www.osha.gov

Guidelines for Retail Grocery Stores

Ergonomics for the Prevention of Musculoskeletal Disorders

U.S. Department of Labor

Elaine L. Chao, Secretary

Occupational Safety and Health Administration

John L. Henshaw, Assistant Secretary

OSHA 3192-06N

2004

I0483150

Contents

Executive Summary

OSHA's *Ergonomics for the Prevention of Musculoskeletal Disorders: Guidelines for Retail Grocery Stores* provide practical recommendations to help grocery store employers and employees reduce the number and severity of injuries in their workplaces. Many of the work-related injuries and illnesses experienced by grocery store workers are musculoskeletal disorders (MSDs), such as back injuries and sprains or strains that may develop from various factors, including lifting, repetitive motion disorders such as carpal tunnel syndrome, or injuries resulting from overexertion. MSDs may also be caused partly or wholly by factors outside of work.

More remains to be learned about the relationship between workplace activities and the development of MSDs. However, OSHA believes that the experiences of many grocery stores provide a basis for taking action to better protect workers. As the understanding of these injuries develops and information and technology improve, the recommendations made in this document may be modified.

Grocery stores that have implemented injury prevention efforts have said they have successfully reduced work-related injuries and workers' compensation costs. Many times, these efforts have reduced injuries and led to increased worker efficiency and lowered operating costs. For example, designing checkstands to reduce ergonomic risk factors such as twisting or extended reaching can improve cashier effectiveness and productivity (1). The purpose of these voluntary guidelines is to build on the progress that the grocery store industry has made in addressing causes of work-related injuries and illnesses.

These guidelines are intended only for retail grocery stores and combined full-line supermarket and discount merchandisers including warehouse retail establishments. The discussion is intended primarily for grocery store managers and store employees, but may also be useful for corporate managers or corporate safety professionals. OSHA did not develop these guidelines to address warehouses, convenience stores, or business operations that may be located within grocery stores, such as banks, post offices, or coffee shops. However, operations in retail or distribution that involve similar tasks or operations as those addressed in these guidelines may find the information useful.

The information in these guidelines provides grocery stores with effective approaches, as well as useful references to be used when determining the need for ergonomic solutions. The recommendations and information presented here are intended as a general guideline and flexible framework to be adapted to the needs and resources of each individual store. OSHA recognizes that small employers, in particular, may not have the need for as comprehensive a program as would result from implementation of every action and strategy described in these guidelines. Additionally, OSHA realizes that small grocery stores may need assistance to implement an appropriate ergonomics program. That is why OSHA emphasizes the availability of its free consultation service for smaller employers.

The heart of these guidelines is the description of various solutions that have been implemented by grocery stores. OSHA recommends that grocery stores consider these solutions in the context of a systematic process that includes the elements described in the pages that follow. Such a process will make it more likely that the solutions implemented in a particular workplace are successful in reducing injuries and are cost effective.

To develop these guidelines, OSHA reviewed existing ergonomic practices and programs in the grocery store industry and conducted site visits to observe existing programs in action. In addition, the Agency reviewed available scientific information regarding work activities that may benefit from ergonomic improvements and specific solutions. OSHA also conducted one-on-one and group meetings with major stakeholder groups to gather the best available information on typical workplace activities and on practices, programs and processes that have been used successfully in the grocery store industry.

Introduction

Grocery stores provide a vital service to the American public, and are a major source of employment in the United States. In recent years, the efforts of grocery store managers and employees have resulted in fewer occupational injuries and illnesses. Even with these efforts, thousands of grocery store workers are still injured on the job each year (2).

Many grocery stores have taken actions such as those recommended in this document to help reduce exposures to ergonomic risk factors in their effort to reduce workplace injuries.

Some grocery store work can be physically demanding. Many grocery store workers handle thousands of items each day to stock shelves, check groceries, decorate bakery items, and prepare meat products. These tasks involve several ergonomic risk factors. The most important of these include force, repetition, awkward posture, and static postures (4).

In the grocery store industry, the presence of these risk factors increases the potential for injuries and illnesses. In these guidelines, OSHA uses the term musculoskeletal disorders (MSDs) to refer to a variety of injuries and illnesses, including:

- Muscle strains and back injuries that occur from repeated use or overexertion;

- Tendinitis;

- Carpal tunnel syndrome;

- Rotator cuff injuries (a shoulder problem);

- Epicondylitis (an elbow problem); and

- Trigger finger that occurs from repeated use of a single finger.

Just because an employee develops an MSD does not mean it is work-related. As required by OSHA's recordkeeping rule (29 CFR 1904), employers should consider an MSD to be work-related if an event or exposure in the work environment either caused or contributed to the MSD, or significantly aggravated a pre-existing MSD. For example, when an employee develops carpal tunnel syndrome, the employer needs to look at the hand and forearm activity required

The Liberty Mutual Insurance Company's Workplace Safety Index shows the importance of ergonomic issues.

The Index lists overexertion, bodily reaction, and repetitive motion as three of the top ten causes of workplace injury.

The three injury categories represented 43.8 percent of the total costs of serious workplace injuries in 2001.

While the total number of serious workplace injuries declined between 1998 and 2001, the cost grew 13.5 percent, or 4 percent after adjusting for inflation (3).

Putting merchandise in the front of a display case improves the appearance of merchandise. However, working in the back of a deep display case to face or stock merchandise can be awkward and uncomfortable, especially when heavy items are involved.

One familiar solution to this problem is display cases that are stocked from the back. The product, such as cartons of milk, slides down an inclined shelf so that it's always in front of the customer. It's also easier for the employee stocking the shelf.

Recently a market extended this concept to front-loaded cases. The solution was a dummy back for the case that was placed at the back of the shelf to limit the reach. Now the merchandise is at the front of the shelf, readily visible to the customer and within easy reach for the worker.

At least one vendor has improved this concept by providing cases with spring-loaded backs. When a customer removes an item, the back pushes the remaining items to the front, keeping them within easy reach. The design makes it easier to stock cases by eliminating the need to reach to the back of the case. The stocker puts the first products in at the front of the shelf, then pushes it back to make room for more items (5).

Packing produce and other products in ice keeps them fresh and appealing. It also means handling ice – shoveling it, lifting it and shoveling it again. It's heavy work and takes time.

Recently a market devised a method to reduce the amount of time that it takes to put ice on products and that also cut the amount of handling in half. Originally an employee took a cart to the ice machine, scooped up enough ice to fill a cart, wheeled the cart to the display case, and finally scooped the ice from the cart into the display case.

The new machine allows gravity flow of ice and has space underneath for a cart containing four buckets. The ice falls into the buckets and fills them, eliminating half the shoveling. The buckets are convenient to handle and can be picked up to pour the ice into the display case, eliminating the rest of the need to shovel. The net result – less strenuous work, more time saved, and an attractive display (5).

for the job and the amount of time spent doing the activity. If an employee develops carpal tunnel syndrome, and his or her job requires frequent hand activity, or forceful or sustained awkward hand motions, then the problem may be work-related. If the job requires very little hand or arm activity then the disorder may not be work-related.

Activities outside of the workplace that involve physical demands may also cause or contribute to MSDs. In addition, development of MSDs may be related to genetic causes, gender, age, and other factors. Finally, there is evidence that reports of MSDs may be linked to occupationally-related psychosocial factors including job dissatisfaction, monotonous work and limited job control (6). However, these guidelines address only physical factors in the workplace that are related to the development of MSDs.

Grocery stores that have implemented injury prevention efforts focusing on musculoskeletal and ergonomic concerns have reported reduced work-related injuries and associated workers' compensation costs. Fewer injuries can also improve morale, reduce employee turnover, encourage employees to stay longer and discourage senior employees from retiring early. Workplace changes based on ergonomic principles may also lead to increased productivity by eliminating unneeded motions, reducing fatigue and increasing worker efficiency. Healthier workers, better morale, and higher productivity can also contribute to better customer service.

These guidelines present recommendations for changing equipment, workstation design, or work methods with the goal of reducing work-related MSDs. Many ergonomic changes result in increased efficiency by reducing the time needed to perform a task. Many grocery stores that have already instituted programs have reported reduced MSDs, reduced workers' compensation costs, and improved efficiency.

A Process for Protecting Workers

Many of the recommendations below are practices taken from workplace ergonomics and safety programs that grocery stores have developed and that OSHA observed while performing site visits at grocery stores. They are intended to provide a flexible framework that a grocery store manager can adapt to an individual store. In many grocery stores, ergonomics, other employee safety and health efforts, workers' compensation, and risk management are integrated into a single program that is usually administered by the same staff. OSHA recommends that employers develop a process for systematically addressing ergonomics issues in their facilities, and incorporate this process into an overall program to recognize and prevent occupational safety and health hazards.

Store and company management personnel should consider the general steps discussed below when establishing and implementing an ergonomics program. It should be noted, however, that each store will have different needs and limitations that should be considered when identifying and correcting workplace problems. Different stores may implement different types of programs and activities and may assign different staff to accomplish the goals of the ergonomics program.

Provide Management Support

Management support for reducing MSDs and communicating support to employees is very important. You have already demonstrated your interest in reducing MSDs by reading these voluntary guidelines. Management support improves the grocery store's ability to maintain a sustained effort, allocate needed resources, and follow up on program implementation. OSHA recommends that employers:

- Develop clear goals,
- Express the company's commitment to achieving them,

- Assign responsibilities (training, job analysis, etc.) to designated staff members to achieve those goals,
- Ensure that assigned responsibilities are fulfilled, and
- Provide appropriate resources.

Meaningful efforts by management also improve employee participation, which is another essential element for achieving success.

Involve Employees

Employees are a vital source of information about hazards in their workplace. Employees help identify hazards and solve problems. Their involvement can enhance job satisfaction, motivation, and acceptance of workplace changes. There are many different ways employers can involve employees in their ergonomics efforts, including the following:

- Submit suggestions and concerns;
- Identify and report tasks that are difficult to perform;
- Discuss work methods;
- Provide input in the design of workstations, equipment, procedures and training;
- Help evaluate equipment;
- Respond to surveys and questionnaires;
- Report injuries as soon as they occur;
- Participate fully in MSD case investigations; and
- Participate in task groups with responsibility for ergonomics.

Identify Problems

It is important to periodically review your job site and the activities of employees to identify possible ergonomic issues. This could include a review of OSHA 300 and 301 injury and illness information, workers' compensation records and employee reports of problems.

You can also identify ergonomic issues by talking with employees and walking through the grocery store to observe employees performing their jobs. When reviewing the various jobs in the grocery store, pay particular attention to the risk factors listed below.

- Force – the amount of physical effort required to perform a task (such as heavy lifting[1], pushing or pulling), handle merchandise, or maintain control of equipment or tools;

- Repetition – performing the same motion or series of motions continually or frequently for an extended period of time;

- Awkward and static postures – assuming positions that place stress on the body, such as prolonged or repetitive reaching above shoulder height, kneeling, squatting, leaning over a counter, using a knife with wrists bent, or twisting the torso while lifting (4); and

- Contact stress – pressing the body or part of the body (such as the hand) against hard or sharp edges, or using the hand as a hammer.

When there are several risk factors in a job, there can be a greater risk of injury. However, the presence of risk factors in a job does not necessarily mean that employees will develop an MSD. Whether certain work activities put an employee at risk of injury depends on the duration (how long), frequency (how often), and magnitude (how intense) of the employee's exposure to the risk factors in the activity (6). For example, performing cashier work for an extended period of time without a break has been associated with increased hand and wrist problems (7) and could contribute to back and lower limb problems (8).

The grocery store industry has developed a number of protocols and checklists to assess work activities. For example, Figures 1 and 2 contain checklists grocery stores may use to help identify ergonomic concerns. The checklists include materials developed by the Food Marketing Institute (4) as well as materials developed by OSHA.

Implement Solutions

Examples of potential solutions for various concerns are located in the Implementing Solutions section of these guidelines.

Address Reports of Injuries

The solutions recommended in these guidelines are intended to address factors that are believed to be associated with MSDs in grocery stores. They are not a guarantee against any future injury occurring. Grocery stores rarely have on-site medical staff to care for injured or ill employees. Therefore, store managers or other designated individuals should establish a procedure for receiving reports of injuries and responding to them appropriately. Early intervention is an effective method of handling potential injuries. Employees should report injuries early so that action can be taken to address any potential job-related issues. Medical treatment and possible work restrictions could be necessary, but attention should be paid to addressing root problems early to avoid more costly actions if injuries are left unaddressed (9, 10, 11).

OSHA's injury and illness recording and reporting regulation (29 CFR 1904) requires employers to keep records of work-related injuries and illnesses. These reports can help the retail grocery store identify problem areas and evaluate ergonomic efforts. Federal and state laws prohibit discriminating against employees who report a work-related injury or illness. 29 U.S.C. 660(c).

(Continued on page 11)

---

[1] There are varying opinions regarding the maximum amount of weight an employee should lift. OSHA does not make a specific recommendation in these guidelines regarding this maximum amount but notes that employers should take into account such considerations as the employees' physical abilities and the number of times a lift must occur. Industry groups such as the Grocery Manufactures of America and Food Marketing Institute encourage the use of containers or packages weighing 40 pounds or less. Another industry group, The International Mass Retail Association, suggests 50 pounds as a maximum weight for lifting.

Figure 1.

If the answer to any of the following questions is **yes**, the activity should be further reviewed.

Force in Lifting

- Does the lift involve pinching to hold the object?
- Is heavy lifting done with one hand?
- Are very heavy items lifted without the assistance of a mechanical device?
- Are heavy items lifted while bending over, reaching above shoulder height, or twisting?
- Are most items lifted rather than slid over the scanner?

Force in Pushing, Pulling, Carrying

- Are dollies, pallet jacks, or other carts difficult to get started?
- Is there debris (e.g., broken pallets) or uneven surfaces (e.g., cracks in the floor) or dock plates that could catch the wheels while pushing?
- Is pulling rather than pushing routinely used to move an object?
- Are heavy objects carried manually for a long distance?

Force to Use Tools

- Do tools require the use of a pinch grip or single finger to operate?
- Are tools too large or too small for the employee's hands?

Repetitive Tasks

- Are multiple scans needed?
- Is a quick wrist motion used while scanning?

- Do repetitive motions last for several hours without a break (e.g., slicing deli meats, scanning groceries)?
- Does the job require repeated finger force (e.g., kneading bread, squeezing frosting, using pricing gun)?

Awkward and Static Postures

- Is the back bent or twisted while lifting or holding heavy items?
- Are objects lifted out of or put into cramped spaces?
- Do routine tasks involve leaning, bending forward, kneeling or squatting?
- Do routine tasks involve working with the wrists in a bent or twisted position?
- Are routine tasks done with the hands below the waist or above the shoulders?
- Are routine tasks done behind (e.g., pushing items to bagging) or to the sides of the body?
- Does the job require standing for most of the shift without anti-fatigue mats?
- Do employees work with their arms or hands in the same position for long periods of time without changing positions or resting?

Contact Stress

- Are there sharp or hard edges with which the worker may come into contact?
- Do employees use their hands as a hammer (e.g., closing containers)?
- Does the end of the tool/utensil (knife) handle press into the worker's palm?

Figure 2.

If the answer to any of the following questions is **no**, the activity may be a potential source of ergonomic concern, depending on the duration, frequency, and magnitude of the activity.

Cashiering

- Are items within easy reach?
- Are keyboard supports adjustable?
- Can the cashier work with items at about elbow height?
- Can the display be read without twisting?
- Are all edges smoothed or rounded so the cashier does not come into contact with sharp or hard edges?
- Are objects easily scanned the first time?
- Are objects scanned without twisting hand motions?
- Can cashiers scan heavy/bulky/awkward items without lifting them?
- Are the scale, conveyor, and horizontal scanner plates all the same height?
- Is the scanner plate clean and unscratched?
- Does the cashier have an anti-fatigue mat and/or footrest?

Bagging and Carry Out

- Can the bagger adjust the height of the bag stand?
- Are all edges smoothed or rounded so the bagger does not come into contact with sharp or hard edges?
- Do bags have handles?
- Can the bagger put bags into cart without leaning over the checkstand or twisting the back?

Produce

- Are knives kept sharp?
- Are worktables, etc. positioned so that the work can be performed at about elbow height?
- Are carts used to move heavy items?

Shelf Stocking & Stockrooms

- Are step stools/ladders used to reach high shelves?
- Is stocking performed with minimal twisting or bending?
- Do totes and boxes have handles?
- Are gloves used for handling cold items?
- Are box cutter blades sharp?
- Are carts used to move heavy items?
- Are carts or pallet jacks used to keep lifts at waist height?
- Are lightweight pallets used?
- Are box weights within the lifting ability of employees?

Bakery

- Are counter heights and widths appropriate for employees?
- Are carts used to move heavy items?
- Are routine job tasks performed without holding hands/wrists in a bent or twisted position?
- Is work being performed at about elbow height?

Meat and Deli Related Tasks

- Are knives kept sharp?
- Are counter heights and widths appropriate for employees?
- Are scales, grinders, slicers, etc. positioned so that the work can be performed at about elbow height?
- Are routine job tasks performed without holding hands/wrists in a bent or twisted position?
- Are box weights within the lifting ability of employees?
- Are tool handles the right size (not too large or too small) for the worker?

(Continued from page 8)

Sometimes the muscle soreness employees experience when starting or returning to a job can be confused with symptoms of MSD injuries. In most cases muscle soreness from conditioning lasts only a few days. Temporary muscle soreness occurs most often with new employees or workers who are returning to a job after several weeks away. When the symptoms linger or gradually get worse, an MSD may be developing.

Provide Training

Training is critical for employers and employees to safely use the solutions identified in these guidelines. Training should be provided in a manner and language that all employees can understand. There are many ways employers can integrate ergonomics training into regular workplace activities, such as new employee orientation or at staff, department, or shift meetings. There are also many sources of training materials, including OSHA, trade associations, and insurance companies. OSHA recommends training for grocery store employees that provides:

- Knowledge of the work tasks that may lead to pain or injury;

- Understanding of the proper tools and work practices for tasks that employees will be performing;

- The ability to recognize MSDs and their early indications;

- The advantages of addressing early indications of MSDs before serious injury has developed; and

- Awareness of the grocery store's procedures for reporting work-related injuries and illnesses as required by OSHA's injury and illness recording and reporting regulation (29 CFR 1904).

OSHA also recommends that management and supervisory staff who coordinate and direct ergonomics efforts receive training to give them the knowledge to effectively carry out their responsibilities. These designated staff members will benefit from information and training that will allow them to:

- Appropriately use checklists and other tools to analyze tasks in the grocery store;

- Address problems by selecting proper equipment and work practices;

- Identify the potential benefits of specific workplace changes;

- Help other workers implement solutions; and

- Assess the effectiveness of ergonomics efforts.

Grocery store employees will also benefit from refresher training to address new developments in the workplace and to reinforce knowledge acquired in the initial training.

Evaluate Progress

OSHA recommends that grocery stores evaluate the effectiveness of their ergonomic efforts and follow-up on unresolved problems. Evaluation and follow-up help sustain continuous improvement in reducing injuries and illnesses, track the effectiveness of specific ergonomic solutions, identify new problems, and show areas where further attention is needed. Grocery managers can use the same methods they use to identify ergonomic concerns (such as OSHA 300 and 301 injury and illness information, workers' compensation records, employee interviews, and observation of workplace conditions) to evaluate progress (10, 11). Employers can also keep a list of activities and improvements to track what has been accomplished and provide data on the effectiveness of the initiatives.

How often an employer evaluates the program will vary by the size and complexity of the facility. Management should revise the program in response to identified deficiencies and communicate the results of the program evaluation and any program revisions to employees.

Implementing Solutions

The section on ergonomic solutions for grocery stores describes changes to equipment, work practices, and procedures that can address ergonomic risk factors, help control costs, and reduce employee turnover. These changes may also increase worker productivity and efficiency because they eliminate unnecessary movements and reduce heavy manual work. OSHA recommends employers use engineering and administrative techniques, where feasible, as the preferred method of dealing with ergonomic issues in retail grocery stores. The first solutions described are those that are applicable to all or most areas of the grocery store. Then, solutions for specific grocery store departments are presented, including:

■ Front end (checkout, bagging and carryout);

■ Stocking;

■ Bakery;

■ Meat and deli department; and

■ Produce department.

OSHA is not providing specific solutions for every department of every grocery store, but the general recommendations should be useful. OSHA expects that a grocery store may need to implement a variety of solutions to address issues in different areas of the store. However, OSHA does not expect all of the solutions to be used in a single grocery store. The solutions are not intended to be an exhaustive list. Grocery store managers are encouraged to develop innovative ergonomic solutions that are appropriate to their workplace. These are only examples of ergonomic solutions which individual store managers should consider as a starting point. Managers are encouraged to look for other innovative methods that will meet their store's needs.

Employers should pay particular attention to ergonomic issues when redesigning existing stores or designing new ones. At that time, major changes are easier to implement and ergonomic design elements can be incorporated at little or no additional cost (12).

King Kullen Grocery Company reported that they initiated a three-fold approach to effectively manage checkout repetitive motion concerns. First, they initiated training for cashiers, store managers and management personnel. They focused training for checkers on awareness of repetitive motion issues, good work practices, and the value of early injury reporting.

Second, King Kullen changed the design of their checkout stations and scanners. The changes included using a combined scanner and scale to reduce lifting and twisting arm motions, and locating the scanner directly in front of the cashier to reduce torso twisting. Finally, King Kullen worked to return injured employees to work as quickly as possible. Under their program, a nurse contacts injured employees within 48 hours of their injury and monitors their care until they return to work.

According to King Kullen, by putting these changes in place, they reduced MSD incidents from 21 in 1992 to 5 in 1996 (13).

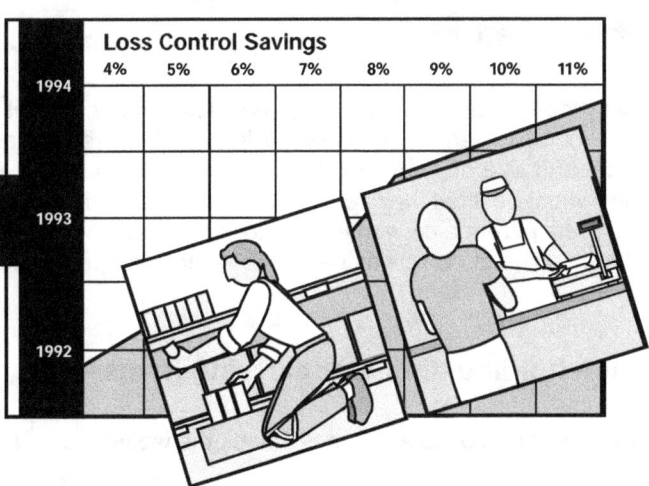

S T O R E W I D E
ERGONOMIC SOLUTIONS

This section describes storewide ergonomic principles on safe work practices employees can follow to reduce their risk of injury. Employers should train employees to use these techniques and design stores to make it easy to do so.

Power Grips

A power grip uses the muscles of the hand and forearm effectively, and is less stressful than a pinch grasp. Consequently, a one- or two-handed power grip should be used whenever possible.

A power grip can be described as wrapping all the fingers and the thumb around the object that is being gripped. It is sometimes described as making a fist around the object being gripped.

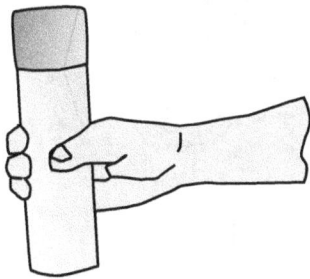

The power grip can be used for many items, including bags, cans and small boxes.

Power Lifts

When the item to be grasped is too heavy or bulky to lift with a one-hand power grip, use the two-hand power grip.

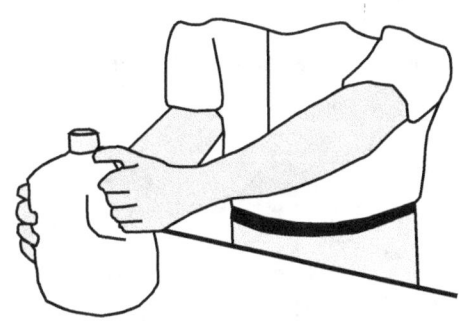

Pinch Grasps

A pinch grasp should never be used when a power grip can be used instead. However, a pinch grasp is acceptable for small, light items (e.g., a pack of gum, etc.).

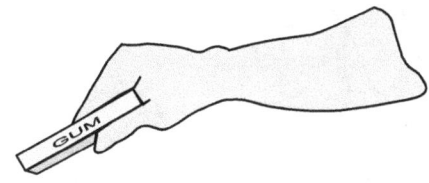

STOREWIDE ERGONOMIC SOLUTIONS

Lifting Safety

Most grocery store jobs involve some lifting. It is important that employers provide employees with help to lift heavy or bulky items. Whether a particular lift will require assistance depends on several factors, including the weight and size of the object, how frequently the object is lifted, how close the object is to the ground, how high it must be lifted, how far it must be carried and whether it has handles. Assistance can include a dolly or cart, or help from a co-worker. Employees should be trained in the use of appropriate lifting techniques for different sizes of objects as well as to when it is appropriate to seek assistance.

When holding, lifting or carrying items

- Before lifting boxes and cases, check the weight so you can prepare to lift properly.

- Turn the body as a unit to avoid twisting at the waist.

- Keep the item close to your body.

- Keep your back straight.

- Use your leg muscles to do the lifting.

- Lift smoothly without jerking.

- Get close to where you want to set the item down.

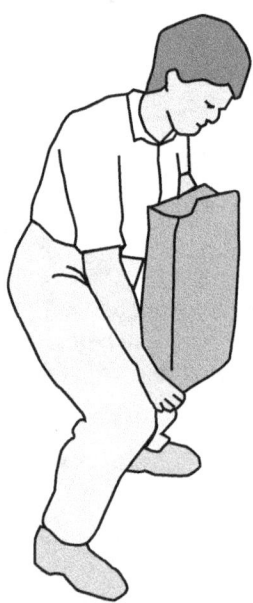

STOREWIDE ERGONOMIC SOLUTIONS

Recommended Working Postures

Recommended Working Postures describe body positions that are neutral and comfortable to use. Using postures other than those recommended will generally waste energy and motion as well as potentially raise the risk of injury. It's also important to change position frequently and stretch between tasks. This improves circulation and lessens fatigue.

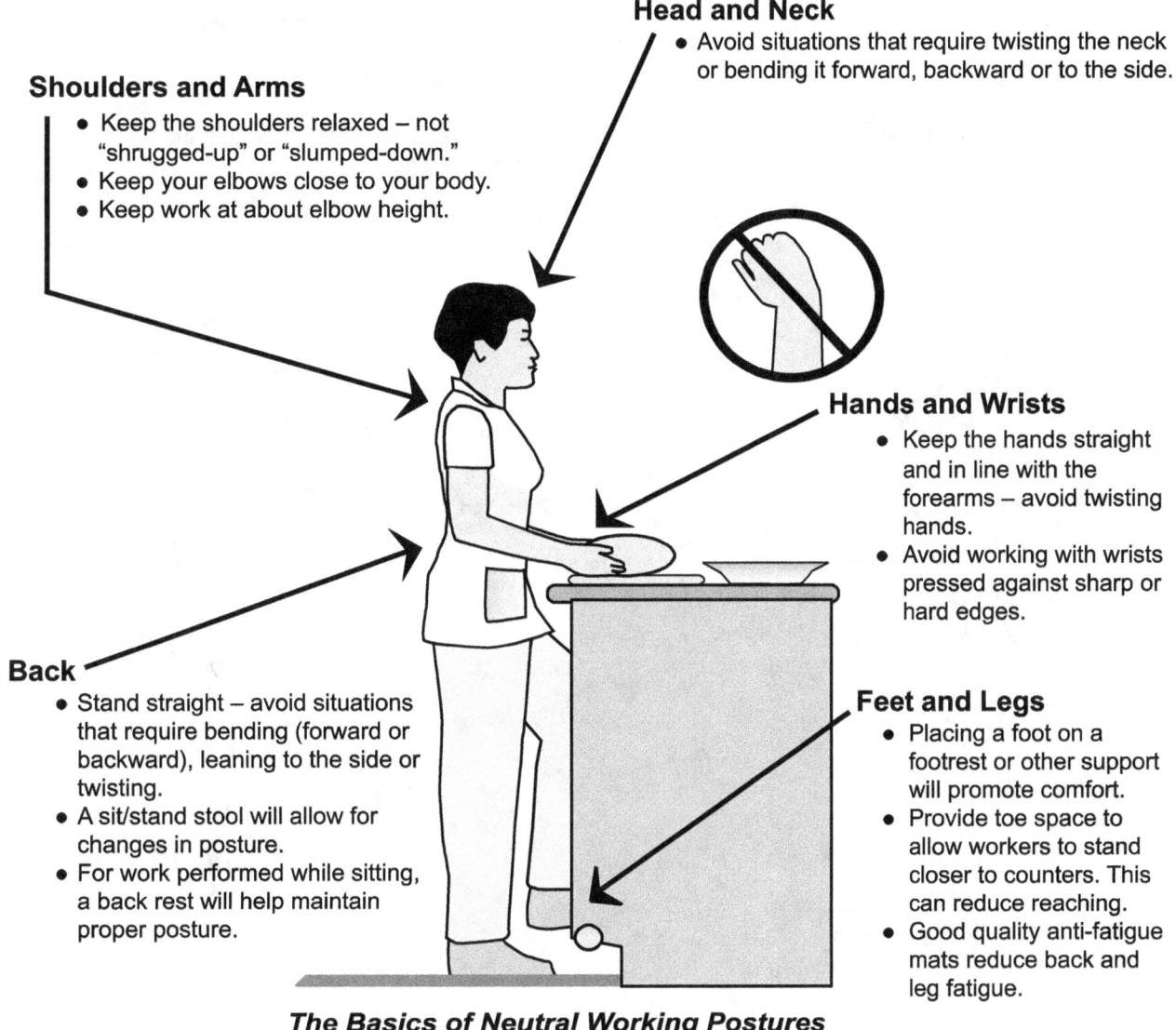

Head and Neck
- Avoid situations that require twisting the neck or bending it forward, backward or to the side.

Shoulders and Arms
- Keep the shoulders relaxed – not "shrugged-up" or "slumped-down."
- Keep your elbows close to your body.
- Keep work at about elbow height.

Hands and Wrists
- Keep the hands straight and in line with the forearms – avoid twisting hands.
- Avoid working with wrists pressed against sharp or hard edges.

Back
- Stand straight – avoid situations that require bending (forward or backward), leaning to the side or twisting.
- A sit/stand stool will allow for changes in posture.
- For work performed while sitting, a back rest will help maintain proper posture.

Feet and Legs
- Placing a foot on a footrest or other support will promote comfort.
- Provide toe space to allow workers to stand closer to counters. This can reduce reaching.
- Good quality anti-fatigue mats reduce back and leg fatigue.

The Basics of Neutral Working Postures

STOREWIDE ERGONOMIC SOLUTIONS

Best and Preferred Work Zones

Performing work within the best and preferred work zones shown below facilitates productivity and comfort. Work is safest when lifting and reaching is performed in these zones. Working outside these work zones results in non-neutral postures that may increase the risk of injury. It is particularly important to perform heavy lifting tasks within the best work zone.

Best Work Zone

- As far forward as your wrist when you hold your arm slightly bent.

- As wide as the shoulders.

- Upper level at about heart height.

- Lower level at about waist height.

Preferred Work Zone

- As far forward as your hand when you hold your arm out straight.

- A foot on either side of the shoulders.

- Upper level at shoulder height.

- Lower level at tip of fingers with hands held at the side.

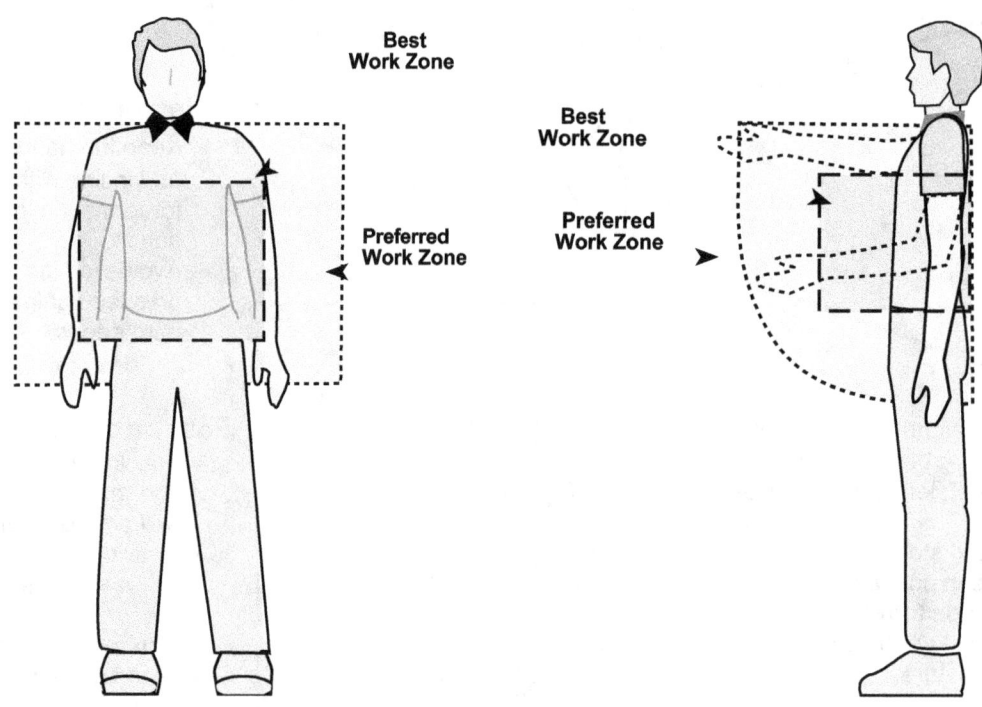

FRONT END
(CHECKOUT, BAGGING AND CARRYOUT)

- Use a powered in-feed conveyor to help cashiers bring the items to their best work zone, rather than leaning and reaching to get items further up the conveyor.

- Use a "sweeper" to move items on the conveyor within the checker's reach.

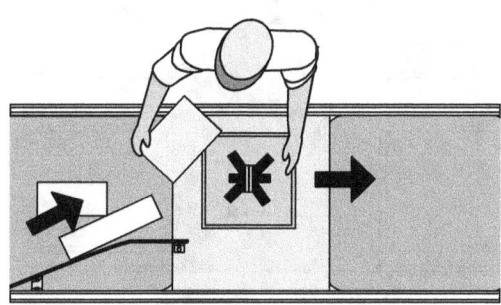

- Locate commonly used items such as the cash drawer and printer within easy horizontal reach.

- Place in-feed and take-away conveyor belts as close as possible to the cashier to minimize reaching.

- Consider using checkstands designed with an adjustable sit/stand or lumbar support against which cashiers can lean.

- Remove, round-off, or pad sharp or hard edges with which the cashier may come into contact.

- Provide footrests for cashiers. Alternately resting the feet helps to reduce fatigue.

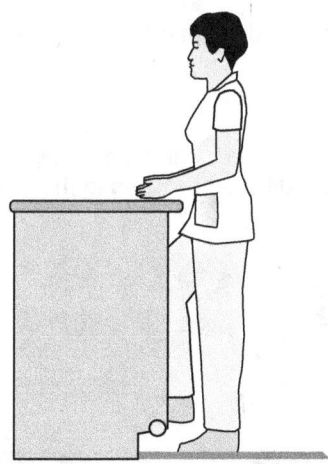

- Provide adequate toe space (at least 4 inches) at the bottom of the workstation. Toe space allows cashiers to move closer to the checkstand, decreasing reaching requirements.

- Use footrests and anti-fatigue mats in areas where workers stand for prolonged periods. Standing on anti-fatigue mats, as compared to bare floors, provides a noticeable improvement in comfort.

- Place the conveyor belt electronic eye close to the scanner, but allow sufficient area between the eye and the scanner to orient items and to ensure the belt does not push items into the scanning field.

- Perform work within the preferred work zone.

- Consider using keyboards to enter the quantity of identical products rather than scanning each individual item.

- Use keyboard to enter code if item fails to scan after second attempt.

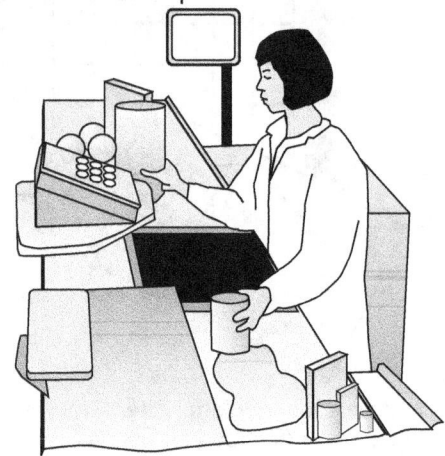

- Place keyboards on supports that adjust in height, horizontal distance and tilt to keep work within the preferred work zone.

- Use front facing checkstands to reduce twisting motions and extended reaches to the side.

- Adjust the checkstand height to match the cashier's waist height, or use a platform.

- Place cash register displays at or slightly below eye level.

- Use scan cards or scan guns for large or bulky items to eliminate the need to handle them.

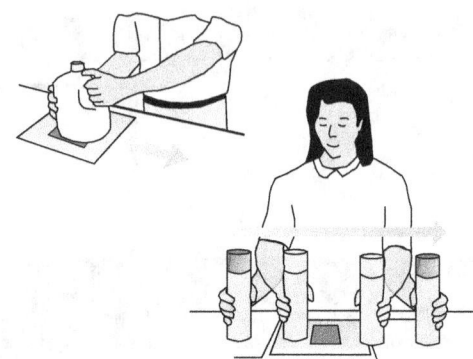

- Set scanners and conveyors at the same height so that cashiers can slide items across rather than lift them.

- Establish a regular maintenance schedule for scanners; clean dirty plates and replace scratched ones.

- Use combined scales/scanners.

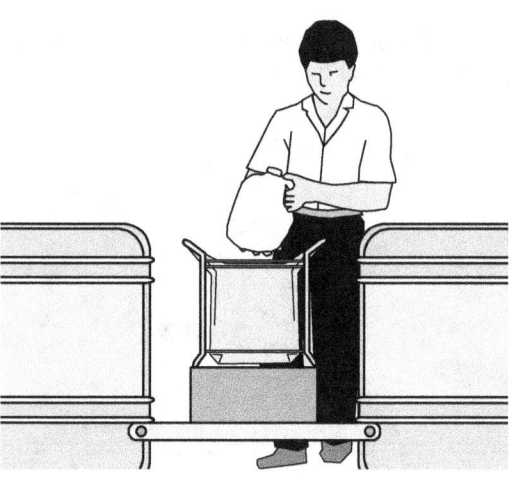

- Provide an adjustable-height bag stand. In bagging areas, the tops of plastic bags should be just below conveyor height.

- To avoid extended reaches when loading bags into carts, move carts closer to the employee.

- Use bags with handles. Handles make the bags easier and less stressful to carry.

- Use carts to carry bags and groceries outside the store.

- Consider using powered-tugs when retrieving carts from the parking area. Powered tugs facilitate moving more carts with more efficiency and less effort.

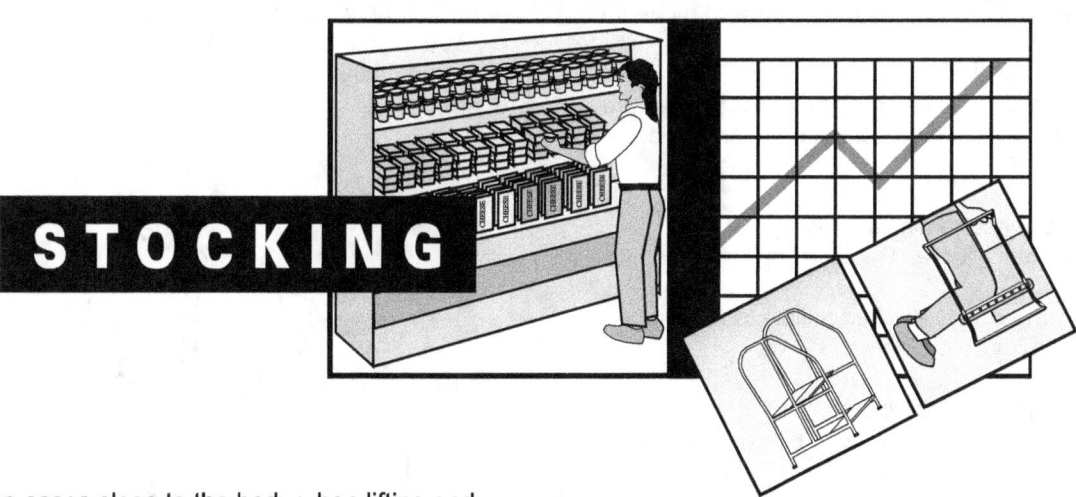

STOCKING

- Keep cases close to the body when lifting and carrying in order to reduce stress to the back.

- Use thermal gloves when stocking frozen foods. Cold temperatures can reduce circulation, causing stress on the hands. If pricing, use a glove with textured fingertips to wipe frost from frozen foods.

- Use a step stool to reach items on the top of pallets or on high shelves.

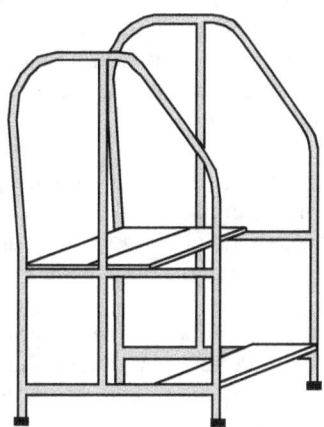

- Use knee pads when stocking low shelves for long periods of time. This reduces the stress on the knees and legs when kneeling.

- Use a kneeler or stool when working at low shelves for long periods of time. This reduces stress on the knees and legs when squatting and kneeling.

- Rotate stocking tasks to avoid prolonged kneeling, squatting, and overhead reaching.

- Use a cart to move items from the pallet to the shelving or case where they are stocked.

- Keep cart wheels well maintained. Wheels that are in poor repair can be difficult to push. Racks or carts with bad wheels should be removed from service until they can be repaired.

- Arrange shelves so that heavy items and fast-moving items are stored within easy reach. This reduces the stress on the body caused by bending or reaching overhead.

- Use the correct safety cutter for the job. Be sure to supply a left-handed cutter if the employee is left-handed.

- Keep safety cutters sharp. Using dull tools requires more force. Replace cutter blades often.

- Report improperly stacked pallets to the supplier to reduce future problems.

- Ensure that the floor areas are level and free of debris and spills. Report any floor problems that need repair immediately.

- Use boxes or totes with hand holds, where suitable.

- Work with suppliers to get lower weight boxes to reduce the weight manually lifted. Industry groups such as the Grocery Manufacturers of America and Food Marketing Institute encourage all companies to use containers and packages that weigh 40 pounds or less (14).

- Use carts with larger wheels so they are easier to push. Use carts with raised bottom shelves so the employee can maintain more neutral body position when lifting or placing cases.

- Ensure that there is adequate room around carts and pallets for lifting tasks. Workers should be able to walk around the pallet or cart, rather than reaching or bending.

- Avoid congestion in grocery store aisles so employees have adequate room to sort cases, open cases, mark merchandise, and stock shelves.

- Equip stockrooms and central processing areas with roller bed conveyors and turntables to reduce lifting and carrying. Maintain turntables so they move easily and with little force required by the worker. Maintain rollers to reduce the pushing and pulling forces needed to handle cases.

- If a turntable is not used, place a flat piece of stainless steel over the end section of the roller bed preferably with a non-stick coating to allow cases to be turned easily. The metal surface should allow the cases to be pushed onto the roller bed easily.

- Use a powered hand jack or scissors-lift to raise the pallet to waist height. This prevents picking up cases with a bent back.

- Work with suppliers to obtain freight with pallet load heights that are within the reach of workers.

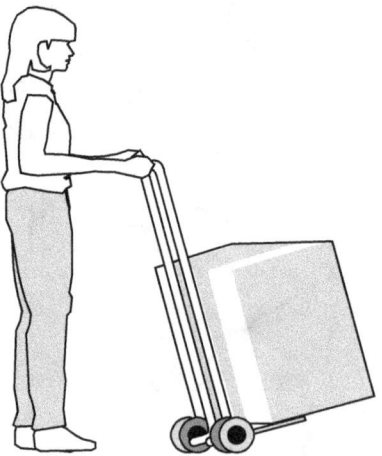

BAKERY

- Position cake-decorating turntables so that the cake is at about elbow height for a more comfortable working position. Adjustable height tables are one solution, but you can also put a riser under the turntable, use turntables with different heights, or put in platforms for shorter people to stand on.

- Use small decorating bags whenever possible to reduce the stress on the worker's hands. The larger the bag, the more force required to squeeze it.

- Have an adequate number of mixing bowls available to reduce the need to transfer icing or batters that are mixed in the store to other containers.

- Use footrests and anti-fatigue mats in areas where workers stand for prolonged periods.

- Make sure that there is toe-clearance under counters and other work surfaces.

- Put buckets of icing and batter on risers (e.g., small stands or empty buckets) to raise them to the best work zone.

- Use smaller containers of flour, sugar, salt and other supplies to reduce the weights that must be handled.

- When lifting keep large bags and containers of ingredients close to the body to reduce stress on the back.

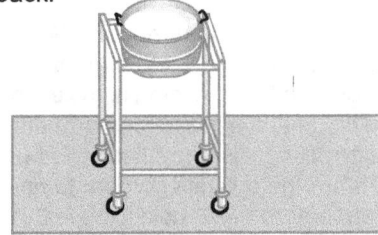

- Use carts or rolling stands to move heavy items like tubs of dough or bags of flour.

- Keep wheels on bakery carts well maintained. Wheels that are in poor repair can be difficult to push and should be removed from service until they can be repaired.

These recommendations are based on information from grocery stores. OSHA recognizes that other bakery operations may be different and that other solutions may be more appropriate for those operations.

- Whenever possible, break up continuous activities such as cake decorating and dough handling with less strenuous tasks during the shift.

- Use a short-handled scoop to put icing into decorating bags. Shorter handles reduce the stress to the wrist.

- Use spatulas, spoons, and other utensils that fit the worker's hand (not too wide or too narrow) and are not slippery.

- Work from the long side of baking pans to reduce reaches when handling dough.

- Use ambidextrous scoops which allow workers to use either hand to dispense dough or batter.

- Use powered mixers whenever possible to mix coloring into icing or purchase colored icing. This reduces the stress to workers' hands and arms from manually mixing colors into icing.

- Ensure that the icing is of correct consistency. Icing that is too thick will be difficult to squeeze through decorating bags. If icing is mixed in the bakery, add liquid to the recipe or warm the icing to obtain the correct consistency. If icing is purchased in buckets, store the buckets at room temperature or warm them before use – cold icing is thicker and hard to squeeze through decorating bags.

- Consider using cake decorating methods that require less use of manual frosting bags. Using an air brush or mechanical dispurser whenever possible can reduce the stress on workers' hands.

- Whenever possible work from the long side of the donut glazing area to reduce reaches and forces on the back. Some glazing stations can be pulled out so that workers can work from the side.

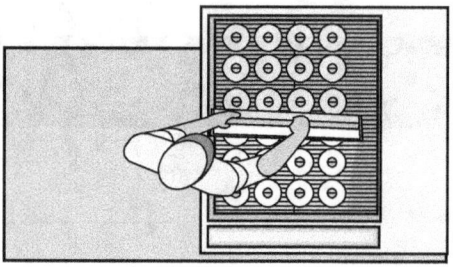

- Use a step stool to reach items on high shelves.

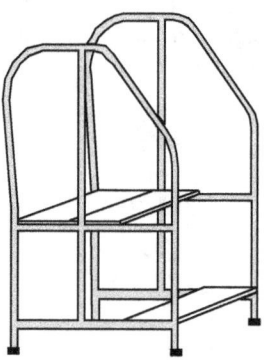

- Look for cases and counter designs that allow the employee to hand customers their selections without high or long reaches.

MEAT & DELI

Many of these solutions may also be useful for the seafood and cheese departments.

- Keep wheels on racks well maintained. Wheels that are in poor repair can be difficult to push. Racks with bad wheels should be removed from service until they can be repaired.

- Keep all grinders, cutters and other equipment sharp and in good repair. Dull or improperly working equipment requires more force to operate.

- Provide thermal gloves for use when handling frozen items.

- Avoid continuous cutting or grinding. Whenever possible, break up these tasks with other, less strenuous tasks throughout the shift.

- Work with suppliers to get meat and other supplies in lower weight boxes to reduce the weight manually handled.

- Keep large boxes and heavy items close to the body. This helps to reduce stress on the back.

- Use a food processor to prepare ingredients for stuffing and other items.

- Arrange the wrapping station so that labels are within easy reach and workers do not have to twist or walk to get to them.

- Remove, round-off, or pad sharp or hard edges with which the worker may come into contact.

- Mount controls of the roller bed close to the wrap station so that workers can reach it easily. If there are two wrap stations, there should be two sets of controls so that neither worker must pull or lug trays down the conveyor.

- Align the roller bed and the wrap station so that employees can slide the trays rather than lift them to the station.

- If overhead storage is necessary, use it for light items such as foam trays.

- Use a step stool to reach items on high shelves.

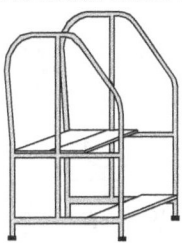

- Position scales so that they can be used in the best work zone. Scales that are too high or too low for a worker can cause employees to work in awkward positions. If possible, make the scale table adjustable so that all workers can work in comfortable postures. Also, position the scale near the lowest part of the counter so that neither the worker nor the customer has to reach over tall deli cases for meat packages.

- Provide a small stool for employees to sit on when catching and traying meat from the grinder. Squatting and bending at the waist can lead to back and leg discomfort, especially when grinding for long periods of time.

- Grind meat into a small lug and move it to a comfortable work surface for traying. This prevents the awkward back posture that results from catching and traying the meat immediately as it leaves the grinder.

- When using tongs select tongs with long handles to reach items in the front of the case.

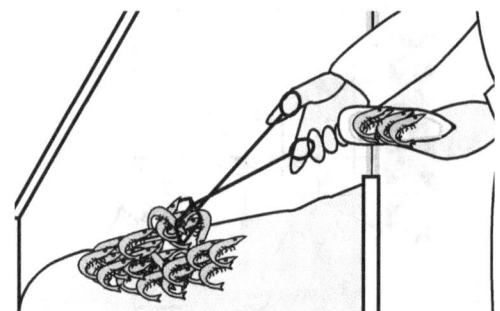

- Whenever possible, work from the long side of trays to reduce reaches and the resultant high stresses on the back.

- Avoid working with the hands/wrists held in a bent or twisted position.

- Keep knives sharp. Workers should be trained in the best knife sharpening methods. Knife sharpening systems should be used regularly, and steels and mousetrap sharpeners should be used to keep knives sharp throughout the shift.

- Try different knives to see if they are more comfortable to use. Some designs work well for specific cutting, trimming, or portioning tasks and should be considered "special purpose" tools.

- Whenever possible, incorporate adjustable work surfaces into the department. Examples include cutting tables, scales and deli slicers.

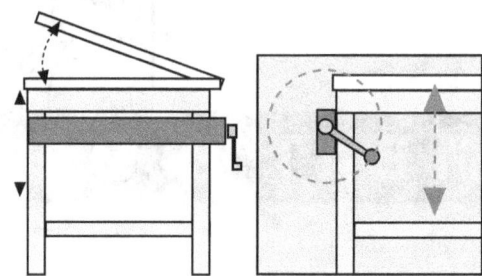

- Look for cases and counters that allow workers to serve customers without excessive reaches.

- Use anti-fatigue mats, footrests, and sit/stand stools where workers are required to stand for long periods of time.

- Look for grinders that do not force the worker to bend over to catch meat or to reach too high to dump meat into the grinder.

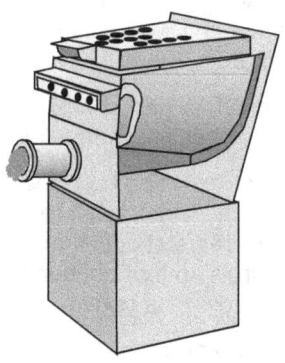

PRODUCE

- Keep manual food processing equipment (knives, slicers, etc.) sharp and in good repair. Equipment that is dull or is not working properly may require excess force to operate.

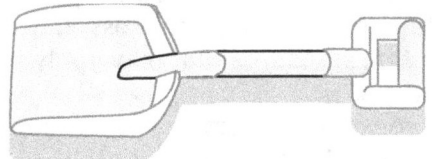

- Use a lightweight shorthandled plastic shovel for ice. This tool is less stressful to the body than heavy shovels. A small shovel allows the worker to move more ice in less time than a hand scoop.

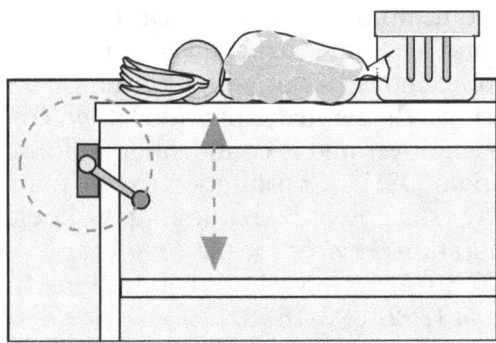

- Use a portable ice case to transfer ice from the ice machine to the produce displays.

- Position scales and wrap stations so that they can be used in the best work zone. Scales that are too high or too low for a worker can cause employees to work in awkward positions. If possible, make the scale and wrap station tables adjustable so that all workers can work in comfortable postures.

- Keep boxes, melons, bags of potatoes, or other heavy items close to the body when lifting and carrying. This helps to reduce stress on the back.

- Keep heavy items, such as watermelons, in shipping containers and use pallet jacks to move them.

- Consider using refrigeration rather than ice to cool produce in order to eliminate the need to shovel ice.

- Place heavier or fast-moving items on shelves that are in the best work zone.

- Use carts to move heavy items; position carts alongside displays to minimize reaching and carrying.

Additional Sources of Information

The following sources may be useful to those seeking further information about ergonomics and the prevention of work-related musculoskeletal disorders in grocery stores.

Working Smart in the Retail Environment Ergonomics Guide, Food Marketing Institute, (202) 452-8444. FMI offers (for a fee) several different guidelines and videos, including this document. This guide instructs cashiers and front line managers how to enhance safety, comfort and productivity. The guide also includes a Working Smart Quick Reference, which summarizes the general and specific techniques employees should use and avoid. (1996, 68 pages)

In Search of Better Checkstands, United Food and Commercial Workers International Union. This document provides detailed information on checkstand design, particularly the advantages of grocery scanners that reduce the need for cashiers to grip and lift grocery items across the scanner.

Easy Ergonomics, A Practical Approach for Improving the Workplace; California Department of Industrial Relations. This document is designed to provide general ergonomics advice and is not industry specific. The document provides a simple, hands-on approach to ergonomics to help employers, supervisors and workers as they work toward improving ergonomic conditions in their workplace. (1999, 90 pages)

Elements of Ergonomics Programs, U.S. Department of Health and Human Services – National Institute for Occupational Safety and Health, (800) 356-4674. The basic elements of a workplace program aimed at preventing work-related musculoskeletal disorders are described in this document. It includes a "toolbox," which is a collection of techniques, methods, reference materials and sources for other information that can help in program development.

Ergonomics for Very Small Business—Retail/ Wholesale (Poster); California Department of Industrial Relations. A poster with examples of safe ergonomic work practices for the very small retail and wholesale employer.

In addition, OSHA's Training Institute in Arlington Heights, Illinois, offers courses on various safety and health topics, including ergonomics. Courses are also offered through Training Institute Education Centers located throughout the country. For a schedule of courses, contact the OSHA Training Institute, 2020 South Arlington Heights Road, Arlington Heights, Illinois, 60005, (847) 297-4810, or visit OSHA's training resources webpage.

There are many states and territories that operate their own occupational safety and health programs under a plan approved by OSHA. Information is available on OSHA's website on how to contact a state plan directly for information about specific state grocery store initiatives and compliance assistance, or different state standards that may apply to grocery stores.

A free consultation service is available to provide occupational safety and health assistance to businesses. OSHA Consultation is funded primarily by federal OSHA but delivered by the 50 state governments, the District of Columbia, Guam, Puerto Rico, and the Virgin Islands. The states offer the expertise of highly qualified occupational safety and health professionals to employers who request help to establish and maintain a safe and healthful workplace. Developed for small and medium-sized employers in hazardous industries or with hazardous operations, the service is provided at no cost to the employer and is confidential. Information on OSHA Consultation can be found at www.osha.gov or by requesting the booklet *Consultation Services for the Employer* (OSHA 3047) from OSHA's Publications Office at (202) 693-1888.

References

(1) Food Marketing Institute. 1992. *Ergonomic Improvement of Scanning Checkstand Designs*. Washington, D.C.

(2) Clarke, Cynthia M., "Workplace injuries and illnesses in grocery stores," *Compensation and Working Conditions*, Bureau of Labor Statistics, December 19, 2003.

(3) Fall 2003 Liberty Mutual Workplace Safety Index: Identifies the direct costs and leading causes of workplace injuries. Liberty Mutual Insurance Company. September 2003.

(4) Food Marketing Institute. 1995. *Working Smart in the Retail Environment – Ergonomics Guide*. Washington, D.C.

(5) E-mail from Supervalu Supermarkets, Inc. to OSHA. 2003.

(6) National Institute for Occupational Safety and Health (NIOSH). 1997. *Musculoskeletal Disorders (MSDs) and Workplace Factors – A Critical Review of Epidemiologic Evidence for Work-Related Musculoskeletal Disorders of the Neck, Upper Extremity and Low Back. National Institute for Occupational Safety and Health (NIOSH) Publication #97-141*. (3-18).

(7) Kennedy, S. et al. 1992. "Prevalence of muscle-tendon and nerve compression disorders in the hand and wrist of a working population of grocery cashiers using laser scanners." Occupational and Environmental Disease Research Unit, University of British Columbia. March 15.

(8) Ryan, G. Anthony, "The prevalence of musculo-skeletal symptoms in supermarket workers," *Ergonomics*, 1989, Vol. 32, No. 4, 359-371.

(9) Cohen, A., C. Gjessing, L. Fine, B. Bernard, and J. McGlothlin. *Elements of Ergonomics Programs*. March 1997. National Institute for Occupational Safety and Health (NIOSH). Publication # 97-117.

(10) Menzel, N. 1994. *Workers' Comp Management from A to Z*. OEM Press. Chapters 11, 12, 19.

(11) Magyar, S. Jr. 1999. "Medical claim management." *Professional Safety*. March.

(12) Hendrick, H. W. 2003, Determining the cost-benefits of ergonomics projects and factors that lead to their success, Applied Ergonomics. 34, 419-427.

(13) Allen, E. 1998. "Keeping grocery checkout lines moving." *Risk Management*. January.

(14) Grocery Manufacturers of America, Food Marketing Institute, Food Distributors International. *Supply Chain Packaging – Voluntary Shipping Container Guidelines for the U.S. Grocery Industry*. 1999.